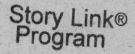

Story Link®
Program

Honeybees are the only domesticated flying insect

Beehives

Jill Kalz

A⁺
Smart Apple Media

COPYRIGHT

Published by Smart Apple Media

1980 Lookout Drive, North Mankato, MN 56003

Designed by Rita Marshall

Copyright © 2002 Smart Apple Media. International copyright reserved in all countries. No part of this book may be reproduced in any form without written permission from the publisher.

Printed in the United States of America

Photographs by Image Finders, Tom Myers, Mary Root, Tom Stack & Associates (John Shaw), Dick Todd

Library of Congress Cataloging-in-Publication Data

Kalz, Jill. Beehives / by Jill Kalz. p. cm. — (Enclosed environments series)

Includes bibliographical references (p.).

ISBN 1-58340-105-9

1. Beehives—Juvenile literature. 2. Honeybee—Juvenile literature. [1. Beehives. 2. Honeybee. 3. Bees. 4. Bee culture.] I. Title.

SF532 .K35 2001   638.1–dc21   00-051582

First Edition 9 8 7 6 5 4 3 2 1

Beehives

Beehive Architecture

Imagine a whole city living in one building. That is just what a beehive is—a home for a large group, or **colony**, of bees—up to 60,000 of them. Beekeepers around the world build hives to collect wax and honey. But they also build them to give honeybees a safe place to live. Beekeepers protect hives from disease, heat and cold, skunks, bears, and other dangers. In ancient times, beekeepers used hollow logs for hives. In places with few trees, they raised bees in clay pots or baskets.

Bees are highly organized insects

Today, most beekeepers use special wooden boxes stacked on top of one another. 🐝 Each box of the hive has a special purpose. The top box is called the honey super. Bees store their extra honey here in sheets of wax called **combs**.

Special glands inside a bee's head make the wax. Each comb is attached to a wood frame and is made of thousands of six-sided rooms, or cells.

Beekeepers harvest honey and sell it in jars or bottles to customers.

Bees fill the cells and seal them with a wax cap. 🐝 The middle box, the food chamber, is also filled with sheets of comb. They hold the bees' main food supply. The colony will feed on

this honey during the cold winter months—sometimes eating

more than 50 pounds (23 kg) in one winter! The bottom

box is called the brood chamber. This is the bee nursery. The

Beekeeping is also called "apiculture"

The first modern beehive was created in 1851

queen bee lays all of her eggs in these cells. After a short time,

the soft, white eggs turn into worm-like **larvae**. The larvae

then spin cocoons and change into **pupae**. During this stage,

pupae start to grow wings, **antennae**, legs, and eyes. When

fully grown, the adult bees chew their way out of the cells. This

whole process is called **metamorphosis**.

Types of Honeybees

Three types of honeybees live in a hive, and they all

have specific jobs. Worker bees are the smallest, measuring

only one-half inch (13 mm) in length. Thousands of worker

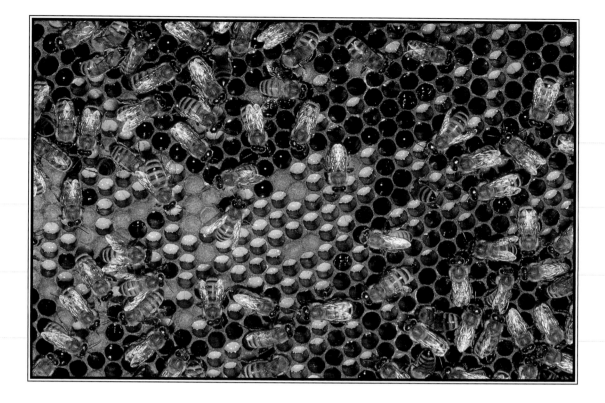

bees do all the chores in the colony. They clean cells, help the

queen bee, feed larvae, build combs, and guard the hive. They

cool the hive in summer by fanning their wings. They keep the

Worker bees make and store honey in combs

hive warm in winter by huddling close together. The worker

bees visit flowers and gather pollen (powdery grains) and nec-

tar (a sweet liquid) to make honey. They even collect plant sap

and use it to seal cracked hive walls. Because **All worker bees are female, but none of them can lay eggs.**

they work so hard, worker bees usually do not

live longer than six weeks. Drones are male

bees. About 100 drones live in a colony. A bit

bigger than worker bees, drones have large eyes, no stinger,

and cannot feed themselves. Drones do not help with any

chores. They have only one job: to mate with a queen bee.

Immediately after mating, drones die. But not all drones get a

chance to mate. 🐝 At three-quarters of an inch (19 mm) in

length, the queen bee is the largest and most important

Bees are very sensitive to movement and scent

honeybee in the hive. Each hive has only one queen, and she

mates only once early in her life. She is the only bee that can

lay eggs, making her the mother of all the bees in her colony.

A small group of worker bees guards her against

enemies and makes sure she is cleaned and fed.

In warm weather, she may lay up to 1,500 eggs

in one day. All of her eggs will develop into

Bees "talk" to one another. They use their antennae to say hello.

worker bees and drones—except the ones fed a yellow syrup

called royal jelly. Those larvae will turn into queen bees.

Beekeepers mark queen bees for quick identification

How Bees Communicate

Bees "dance" on the comb to show other bees where flowers are. Their body movements and dance speed combine to explain the flowers' location and distance from the hive.

Bees also use their sense of smell to communicate. Each time a worker bee touches the queen bee, she picks up the queen's scent and carries it with her throughout the hive. This scent lets the colony know that the queen is healthy and all is well.

When a hive becomes overcrowded, the queen bee and

Swarming usually happens in late spring

half of the colony leave to find a new home. This is called swarming. Worker bees in the old hive then raise new queens by feeding royal jelly to some of the larvae. Each hive can have only one queen, so the first queen out of her cell quickly kills the others. After her wings have developed, she flies high into the air and mates. Soon the brood chamber will be filled with her eggs, and a new colony will begin.

In the fall, any drones still living in the hive are forced out and left to die in the cold of winter.

Honey is an important food product

Getting the Message Right

Good communication is very important in a beehive. Worker bees tell each other where food is. They alert the hive to danger. They share news about the queen. Pretend you and your friends are bees and see how well you can pass messages to each other.

What You Need

A group of friends (more than six works best)

What You Do

1. Gather in a circle.

2. Whisper the following message to the "bee" on your right. You can say it only once, so be clear.

> Worker bees buzz and buzz but will not sting
> unless their hive is in danger. Queen bees have
> stingers too but sting only other queens.

3. Continue passing the message around the circle, "bee" by "bee," until everyone has heard it.

What You See

When the final "bee" repeats the message out loud, you will see how well you and the other "bees" communicated. Did you get the message right?

Beekeepers may rent out bees to pollinate crops

INFORMATION

Index

Words to Know

antennae (an-TEN-ee)—the pair of feelers on the heads of some insects

colony (KOL-eh-nee)—a group of similar creatures living together

combs (KOMES)—bee-made wax structures of thousands of six-sided cells used to hold larvae and honey

larva/larvae (LAR-va; plural LAR-vay)—bees in the worm-like stage of development between egg and pupa

metamorphosis (met-uh-MOR-fuh-siss)—the change in appearance and habits some insects go through from egg to adult

pupa/pupae (PEOO-pa; plural PEOO-pay)—bees in the stage of development between larva and adult

Read More

Cole, Joanna, and Bruce Degen. *The Magic School Bus: Inside a Beehive.* New York: Scholastic Inc., 1998.

Julivert, Angels. *The Fascinating World of Bees.* New York: Barron's Educational, 1991.

Internet Sites

The Beekeeper's Home Pages
http://ourworld.compuserve.com/homepages/Beekeeping/

The National Honey Board Kids' Page
http://www.honey.com/kids/

I BM CyberBee.net HUMANS
http://www.cyberbee.net/

BEES OPERATORS OF CYBER